SAYYIDAH AAISHA :
AGE AND MARRIAGE

SAYYIDAH AAISHA : AGE AND MARRIAGE

WRITTEN BY QAZI FAZL ULLAH

EDITED BY EVELYN THOMPSON

HUND INTERNATIONAL PUBLISHING

LOS ANGELES, CALIFORNIA

2018

First Printing: 2018

ISBN: 978-1-970049-04-6

HUND INTERNATIONAL PUBLISHING
LOS ANGELES, CALIFORNIA
PRINTED IN THE UNITED STATES OF AMERICA

TABLE OF CONTENTS

INTRODUCTION

Islam is a Natural *Deen* or *Deen* of Nature. This is a balanced *Deen* providing a comprehensive justice system, and the *Holy Prophet Muhammad* is the perfect role model as a perfect human. His words, *actions*, and sanctions are the proper interpretation of the *Holy Quran* and the second fundamental source of laws in *Islam*. There is a commonly held belief, especially among critics of *Islam*, that the Prophet *Muhammad* married *Aaisha* when she was only nine years of age. In this book, all the details about this issue is given that how this word *Tis'aa* (which means nine) happened there and what the real story is to counter the false accounts and correct the record.

Allah said:

> *"The same way we made for every prophet enemies from criminals, but enough is your Lord as a guide and as a helper (19:31)."*

"And the same way we had made for every prophet enemies, Satan's among humans and Jinns [demons] they inspire each other decorated words in delusion and if your Lord would have willed they would never have done it so ignore them and their fabrications. And this is so the hearts of those who disbelievers in the last day may incline towards this (deceptive speech) and to like it and let them do what they are doing (6:112)."

Opposition to something or someone usually derives from either ignorance or arrogance. Ignorance can be addressed, and the issue resolved, but arrogance, even if it is addressed, may not be resolved.

WHY?

Because arrogance is based upon some interest, so as long as that interest has not been sacrificed, it cannot be resolved. *Allah* said, regarding Jewish people in the time of the *Prophet Muhammad* when they refused to accept the message of the *Prophet* even though before his birth and message they had been eagerly waiting for him, that when he came and conveyed the message they rejected it,

"You can never avail Iman (belief) until you spend (sacrifice) what you love (3:92)."

And they were in love with wealth and power based on their perverted form of religion and evil practices, and the *Prophet* used to reject these two and calling for the form of *Deen*. He would also call towards no action on evil practices, so they became arrogant and spread rumors about him and his message. They also made up lies to defame the *Prophet* in cooperation with his enemies.

An example is when the prophet married *Zainab Bint Jah'sh*, his first cousin, after she was engaged to *Zaid Ibn Thabit*, the adopted son of the *Prophet Muhammad*. *Zaid* divorced her before the marriage was consummated, and this marriage of her to the *Prophet Muhammad* took place upon the heavens and was solemnized by *Allah*.

As *Allah* said,

> *"And when Zaid was no longer in need of her, we married her to you in order that there may not be upon the believers any discomfort (guilt) concerning the wives of their claimed (adopted) sons when they are no longer in need of them (33:37)."*

After this the hypocrites with the support of the *Bannu Qurayza, Bannu Nadeer, and Bannu Qanuqa* tribes started a rumor that, what a messenger who married his daughter-in-law, (in their culture before *Islam* adopted sons were considered as close as biological ones), and as the wife of a biological son is forbidden to his father, so is the case of the wife of an adopted son.

But in *Islam* this was not the case, and this whole procedure of the *Nikah* (marriage) of *Zainab* to *Zaid*, then his divorce and then her marriage to the *Prophet*, was to nullify this outdated custom. Enemies have nothing to do with reality; rather they are looking for some gray area and loopholes to put their hands in and pull the matter towards their own agenda.

9

As *Allah* said,

> *"Muhammad is not the father of any man amongst you but (he is) the Messenger of Allah and the seal of the prophet (33:40)."*

Which means that if *Zaid* is a man and *Muhammad* does not have a son, then from whence came the daughter-in-law and the prohibition?

Also, in the expedition to the *Muraisee* fountain, his wife *Aaisha* was left behind while looking for a lost necklace, in the company of a man named *Safwan Ibn Mu'attal*. So, he took *Aaisha* on his camel and joined the army, then the hypocrites again started up the rumor mill again and put false charges against them both, only to harm the Prophet and stop his mission. *Allah* himself related the purity and piety of *Aaisha* in *Surah Nur*.

Allah said,

> *"Verily those who brought forth this false fabrication is a group amongst you, do not think it as bad for you (from all angles) but that is good for you (from certain angles) (24:11)."*

This was during the lifetime of the *Prophet* and as he is the last and final *Prophet* of *Allah* for the whole world, and as a known fact we know that every great man has lots of supporters, but also has so many opponents and enemies. Especially when his ideology is a challenge to the ideologies of others, then they propagate against him, make conspiracies, looking for loopholes to use it for their own purpose and agenda.

For a long time, this has been propagated that the *Prophet* married a girl of nine years old. In the West, most laws specify the age of consent as somewhere between 15 and 18 depending on the jurisdiction. But as we know that in different countries there are different rules and laws for different issues, where their culture, customs, and religion also have an influence.

Now this issue of the age of *Aaisha* at the time of her marriage needed thorough research, so we tried to our best to bring forth;

i.   The religious concept about marriage that when it is allowed to be solemnized;

ii. Puberty which is the basic requirement for marriage, but whether it is a permission for its legality and lawfulness or that is an order,

iii. The age of *Aaisha* at her marriage time and analysis of the *Riwayah* (narration) which has mentioned it as nine years old.

May *Allah* make it useful for all those who are looking for truth, *Amin*.

QAZI FAZL ULLAH

LOS ANGELES, CALIFORNIA

UNITED STATES OF AMERICA

MANKIND AND THE MESSAGE

Allah created the world and he created mankind as his *Khaleefah* (agent). For this purpose, he gave him intellect and subjected to him the world and the things therein.

Allah said:

> *"And indeed we have honored the children of Adam and we have given them authority in land and sea, and provided them with good things and preferred them over many of what we created with a specific preference (17:7)."*

> *"Have you not seen (noticed) that Allah has made subject to you whatever is in the heavens and whatever is in the earth and amply bestowed upon you his favors, the apparent one and the unapparent one (31:20)."*

> *"Allah is that one who has created the heavens and the earth and sent down water from the heaven thereby to produce fruits as a provision for you, and he subjected to you the ships to sail therein the sea with his leave, and subjected to you the rivers and he has (also)*

subjected to you the sun and the moon pursuing their courses, and he subjugated to you the night and the day, and he has provided for you all that you need. Verily man is very unjust, ungrateful (14:32-34)."

As we know and this is logical and reasonable that when someone attains status and position and he utilizes its facilities, he becomes bound to certain duties and responsibilities. When he performs those responsibilities, he not only justifies his position but also reaps more and more benefits. A promotion in his status is given, and an increase in compensation as well. Otherwise he would be responsible for this use and would be punished.

HOW CAN HE JUSTIFY THIS?

As we know, if the duty is a professional one, then one needs a proper qualification, training, and learning for the purpose. And if the duty is mechanically practical, then one not only needs a book, which teaches the mechanical functions theoretically or even with diagrams, but an expert to provide practical training. Otherwise the people concerned will not only be unable to perform their duty or do their job, but they will also destroy the equipment involved. And they will not only lose their job, but in some cases they would be punished as well.

Since this whole world has been subjugated to humans and their creator wanted them to perform their duties properly and to obey their Lord, through this concept they will fulfill their needs and necessities in a lawful way and get nearer to *Allah*. Which means satisfaction in this life and prosperity in the hereafter and as a known fact good is meant and needed in this life and in the hereafter.

But as we know that *Allah* is the creator and we are the creation, He is the Lord and Master and we are the slaves. He is the utmost High and we are very ordinary and at a very low status.

Now how can this lowly creation be able to get nearer and closer to that utmost High entity and authority?

Allah said,

> *"O you who believed! Be dutiful to Allah, seek Wasee-lah towards him and strive hard in his path, so you may be successful (5:35)."*

In this verse *Allah* mentioned three things:

(i) Be dutiful to *Allah*

(ii) Seek *Waseelah* towards him

(iii) Strive hard in his path, and the result is success.

Here, number two should be interpreted as being dutiful and striving hard are

(i)   a *Waseelah*,

(ii)   through *Waseelah* one can find out how he can be dutiful and strive hard. So, lets know what *Waseelah* is.

Waseelah literally means

(i)   *means*

(ii)   *"means,"* like a car or a train is a *Waseelah* to take you to the place you want. A job is a *Waseelah* to obtain money. Being obedient and dutiful can get you closer to the boss.

Only *Allah* can tell us and show us the means to get you close to Him. In brief we can say that to get close to *Allah* is to obey him in all that He wants. Now the question is, what does He want?

To this end, He sent the *Prophets* and Messengers. They were created by *Allah* for this specific purpose, and they had a strong but very transparent nature, which one cannot obtain through his own efforts but only through the selection of *Allah*. When *Allah* chose someone to receive his message and to convey it, He made and manufactured that messenger for that specific mission,

As *Allah* said regarding *Musa* (Moses).

"And I have manufactured you for myself (my duty) (20:41)."

Allah also said,

"And so you may be manufactured under my eye (supervision) (20:39)."

That is why almost every messenger did not develop under his father, but rather under the eye of *Allah*. If we consider the history of a few of them, we will see that *Ibrahim* (Abraham) was turned out of the house by his father, when his father said to him,

> *"And if you stop not then I will for sure stone you and get away from me for a long while (forever) (19:46)."*

Also, the son of *Ibrahim*, *Ismail* (Ishmael), was brought along with his mother *Hajar* (Hagar) from the *Holy Land* to *Makkah* by *Ibrahim*, where there was nobody living and no material life was there to exist. In those circumstances *Ismail* developed under the eyes of *Allah*.

Prophet Musa (Moses) was developed in the house of *Fir'un* (Pharaoh), the enemy of his people *Bani Israel* (*Children of Israel*). *Prophet Isa* (Jesus) was born without a father and was developed under the eye of *Allah*.

The *Prophet Muhammad* was an orphaned at a young age. His father passed away two to three months before his birth, so the *Prophet Muhammad* also developed under the eyes of *Allah*.

These Messengers passed through many hardships before receiving the message for about 40 years. So why the hardship? It was the *Waseelah*, the means to get strength, courage, forbearance, patience, stability, and the transparency and purity of their nature to receive the message. Not everyone has the capacity to receive the message. The character of these men was exemplary and they were known for that. As the *Prophet Muhammad* was known and recognized as *As Sadiqul Amin*, the truthful and the trustworthy.

The people of *Prophet Salih*, who was sent to the People of *Thamud*, a tribe in the valley of *Hijr*, said to *Salih*,

> *"They said, O Salih you amongst us were the center of our hopes before this (call and talk of yours) (11:62)."*

WHY WAS THIS?

So people may not have any objections or reservations concerning their character and this is because *Allah* has made them a role model for mankind. They must be truthful in their words and correct and honest in their actions.

Allah said:

> *"Indeed there is for you in Ibrahim (Abraham) a beautiful example (role model) and also in those who were with him (60:4)."*

> *"Indeed, for you there is a beautiful example in them, for those who expect (fear) Allah and whosoever turns away, then Allah is not in need, worthy of all praises (60:6)."*

> *"Indeed there in the Messenger of Allah (Mohammad) is a beautiful example (role model) for one who expects (fears) Allah and the last day (33:21)."*

Expecting *Allah* and the last day means we must believe in meeting with *Allah* on the *Day of Judgment* where everyone will be held accountable.

Also, *Allah* said:

> *"By the star when it goes down, your companion (Mohammad) is neither astray nor being misled. Nor does he speak of (his) desire. It is but revelation, been revealed (53:1-4)."*

When a messenger is a role model for people, then he must be a human, having all the needs and requirements that humans have, as others have to learn from his words and actions, in order to know what to do, to be obedient to *Allah*, and to get closer to him. That is why these messengers are, went to the markets, got married, had children, and lived otherwise normal lives, and when their opponents objected to that, *Allah* answered that objection.

Allah said:

> *"And they said, what sort of a messenger is this who eats food and walks through the markets (25:7)."*

Allah said:

> *"And we have not sent before you the messengers but they used to eat food and to walk in the markets and we have make you a test for each other (25:20)."*

Allah said:

19

"Indeed we sent messengers before you and gave them wives and children (13:38)."

Because an angel does not have the same needs as humans, so he could not be a role model for human beings.

Allah said:

"Say if there were settled on earth angels living satisfactorily, then for sure we would have sent to them from the heaven an angel as a messenger (17:95)."

Allah said:

"And if we would have made him (the messenger) an angel, then for sure we would have made (transformed) him to a man and then we would have caused them confusion as they have been (already confused therein) (6:9)."

Now as the *Prophet Muhammad* is the last and final *Prophet* of *Allah* for the whole world. He has lots of followers, but in the same way he has lots of enemies as well. So his enemies propagate against him that he married *Aaisha* when she was only nine years of age, and that is a child's age according to the western concept.

AHADITH MENTIONING ISSUE OF

MARRIAGE

In this regard we have to mention the narrations by *Imam Bukhari* from:

1.

MOHAMMAD IBN YUSUF

Mohammad Ibn Yusuf, from *Sufyan*, from *Hisham*, from his father *Orwah*, from *Aaisha* that the *Prophet* did *Nikah* with her and she was of six years and consummated the marriage when she was of nine years and she stayed with him nine years.

2.

MU'ALLA IBN ASAD

Mu'alla Ibn Asad, from *Wuhaib*, from *Hisham*, from *Orwah* (his father), and he from *Aaisha*, that the *Prophet* married her when she was six years of age and consummated her marriage when she was nine years of age and that she was with him for nine years.

3.

FARWAH IBN ABIL MAGRA

Farwah Ibn Abil Magra, from *Ali Ibn Mus'hir*, from *Hisham*, from his father, from *Aaisha*, that the *Prophet* married me so my mother came to me and took me to the house of the *Prophet*....

4.

QABEESAH IBN OQBAH

Qabeesah Ibn Oqbah, from *Sufyan*, from *Hisham*, from *Orwah*, from *Aaisha* that the *Prophet* married me, so my mother came to me and took me to the house of the *Prophet*.

5.

IMAM ABU DAWUD

Imam Abu Dawud narrated, from *Sulaiman Ibn Harb* and *Abu Kamil*, they both narrated from *Hammad Ibn Zaid*, from *Hisham*, from *Orwah*, from *Aaisha* that the *Prophet* did *Nikah* with me and I was six and consummated the *Nikah* when I was nine.

WHAT *ISLAMIC SHARIAH* SAYS

In *Shariah* it is mentioned that this is permissible for a father or grandfather to do the *Nikah* of a minor girl, but as we know this is called *Walayah* (guardianship) and in *Shariah* it is mentioned as a legal maxim that

> *"Guardianship depends on good (of the ward for example)."*

That is why the *Shariah* said that mostly the father and grandfather are naturally very compassionate regarding their children so they always have their best interests at heart. As they are experienced due to their age, and do not want to miss a golden opportunity for their daughter, in some circumstances they do their *Nikah* in a minor age. but if this act of theirs was apparently unjust towards the girl, then the state and judiciary can take an action in this regard. Also the girl, after she attains puberty, can go to court and if the action is proven unjust then the court can dissolve that *Nikah*. While in the case of other guardians, like the uncle or brother, if the girl went to the court after she got puberty and asked for dissolution without any reason, then the court will dissolve that *Nikah* as there is another legal maxim that

"Any action which either brings disadvantage or prevents an advantage is forbidden."

AGE OF PUBERTY

In *Shariah*, puberty is known basically through some type of signs, which are menarche in girls and nocturnal emissions (wet dreams) in boys. If none of those signs are there, then age is the basis for puberty, and in this regard, the authentic jurists, who have been followed by the *Ummah* in general, have different opinions.

Imam Shafi and *Imam Ahmad* agree that the age of puberty for both boys and girls is fifteen years. *Imam Malik* said eighteen years for both, and *Imam Abu Hanifah* said eighteen for boys and seventeen for girls. They mentioned that there are some exceptional cases where a girl's menses starts when she is nine years of age or a boy has a wet dream when he is twelve years of age, but these are very rare cases.

According to *Shariah*, marriage may not be consummated until after puberty. There are verses of *Quran* and *Ahadith* of the *Prophet Muhammad* that encourage marriage, but there are others who say otherwise.

Allah said:

"So marry what is permissible for you of the women (4:3)."

And the *Prophet Muhammad* said:

"Marriage is my sunnah (way of life) so whosoever refrained from my sunnah, then he is not from my Ummah (followers)."

But *Allah* also said:

"And those who do not find the means for marriage they may abstain from until Allah enriches them from his bounty (24:33)."

Also the *Prophet Muhammad* said:

"O group of youth whosoever can afford the boarding (lodging i.e. fulfill the obligations) then he should marry as this is a lowering for the eye sight and protector for the private parts, and whosoever cannot then he may fast as this is a shield for him (Bukhari)."

Thus, if a girl married on her own before the age of puberty then it is null and void, and if she did the same after she attained the age of puberty, then according to *Malik, Shafi,* and *Ahmad,* that is also void. But according to *Abu Hanifah* the *Nikah* contract is done as she can make other contracts as well, but a *Nikah* is much more than a sale and purchase contract as it is,

(i) A lifetime contract in *Islam*, and

(ii) This contract does not connect only two people to each other, but rather it connects two families and the offspring as well.

Islam does not want any family breakups, so it said that the guardian has an important position in this regard, so in such a case if he does not have any objection to that marriage of the girl, then that is all right, otherwise he can object to it in a court of law.

THE *PROPHET* MARRIED BASED ON

AN ORDER

The *Prophet* of *Allah* was a human, and a perfect one in each and every aspect. He had all the needs of life as any other human and he was availing and fulfilling that but in a very good and exemplary way. Marriage was his need and natural requirement as well, but was he a slave to his desires?

Not at all; he was

(I)   One who was known for his noble character even before Prophethood and got the title of *As Sadiqul Amin*, the truthful and trustworthy, how can he be enslaved by his desires after he became a Messenger.

(II)   One who was first married when he was a young man of twenty-five years of age to a lady who was forty, and she was a widow of two husbands; how can he be blamed for enslavement by his desires, as someone of such a young age is looking for a young virgin girl?

(III)   As long as his first wife, *Khadijah*, was alive, he never married a second time. When she died the *Prophet Muhammad* was fifty-one years old, then he married another widow named *Saudah Bint Zama'ah* and as long as he was in *Makkah* he never married another one, but when he migrated to *Madinah* and established the first ever *Islamic* State, he was in need of people to learn from him every aspect of life according to *Shariah*, and to also have their lives in accordance with *Shariah*, and to convey the same to others as well. So outside of his house there were so many companions preserving his every word and action, but inside the house he needed people to watch and listen to him. As we know strangers cannot stay inside other's homes even though they are women. As every single minute of the *Prophet's* life was a source of law and *Shariah*, certain aspects of life are known only to one's spouse, and that is also a big part of *Shariah*. Therefore, he needed a few students to live in his house to preserve his words, actions, and activities, so they can convey them to the *Ummah*. By the grace of *Allah*, the wives of the *Prophet* did it in a very exemplary way. *Aaisha* herself narrated more than two thousand *Ahadith*, and almost every wife of the *Prophet* preserved *Ahadith* and narrated the same. As this was based on the order of *Allah* to them.

Allah said:

"And remember (memorize/understand) what is recited in your house of the verses of Allah and the

Hikmah (Ahadith). Indeed Allah is ever subtle, well acquainted (33:34)."

THE CALENDAR AND *ARAB* CULTURE

Humans passed through different evolutionary stages. These stages were different in different zones. Arabs at the time of the *Prophet* were known for their poetry, prose, and their genealogical record-keeping. But they had more than ten different calendars. They were not that much alert about birth dates and as we know that in a case a paper was presented to *Umar* as a proof where the month was written without any date and year, so he asked what year and there was no answer. So after this incident he started the *Hijri* calendar from the migration of the *Prophet*.

Let us have a few references that show accurate dates were not the culture at that time.

1.

As we mentioned before that at the time of marriage *Khadijah* was 40 years of age, but in different books her age is different.

(A) *ZURQANI*

Zurqani referring to *Abbas* the uncle of the *Prophet*, that the time of her marriage *Khadijah* was 28 to 30.

(B) *IBN KATHIR IN AL - BIDAYAH*

Ibn Kathir in Al-Bidayah mentioned that at the time of death, *Khadijah* was 65, but it is also said she was 50.

(C) *BAYHAQI*

Bayhaqi narrated from *Hakim* that she was 25 to 35 at the time of her marriage.

(D) *IBN ISHAQ*

Ibn Ishaq is considered the first compiler of the *Seerah* (biography of the *Prophet*) and *Ibn Hisham* is the second one and *Ibn Hisham* also mentioned 25 to 35.

Here we do not do any research about the age or birthdate of *Khadijah*, but we only indicate that there was neither an established system of calculation nor any record about birthdate or age. That is why these differences are there, and this difference may also be considered regarding the date of the birth of *Fatima*. *Abbas* had told *Fatima* that she was born the year *Quraish* were building the *Kaaba*. At that time the *Prophet* was 35 years of age (*Ibn Sad & Usd l Ghabah*), which means that they were referring mostly to big events.

2.

Saudah, the second wife of the *Prophet*, passed away in year 54 after *Hijrah* according to *Waqidi*, but *Bukhari* narrated in *At Tareekh Ul Kabeer* that she passed away in year 23 after *Hijrah*.

3.

Abbas says that the *Prophet* stayed in *Makkah* as a messenger for fifteen years and he passed away when he was 65 (*Tabari*), while all the scholars say the time in *Makkah* was 13 years and he passed away at the age of 63. It means that *Abbas* counted the birth and death years as complete years.

4.

As we know, the event of ascension was a big event, but still regarding its year there is a difference.

(I) QURTUBI

Qurtubi narrated from *Musa Ibn Oqbah* that it happened six months before *Hijrah*.

(II) KHADIJAH

Khadijah passed away in the seventh year of Prophethood (*Zuhari*), and *Aaisha* said that prayers became mandatory after her death. And we know this was at the time of ascension.

(III) IBN QASIM ZAHABI

According to *Ibn Qasim Zahabi*, ascension occurred eighteen months after he received the first revelation.

Now it does not mean there is any confusion about this event, but only that *Arabs* were not accustomed to keeping and preserving the dates, months, or even years.

5.

This is also disputed amongst the historians whether *Aaisha's Nikah* (betrothal) took place in the tenth year after the message or in the 13th year, a little before *Hijrah*. And also whether the consummation took place in the first year after *Hijrah* or in second year.

Now all these differences are because *Arabs* used to refer certain things or occasions to the year of a big event. For example, they used to say it happened two years before the year of the Elephant, or they would say this happened three years after the year of the Elephant.

Before we go into the relevant *Hadith* and to discuss the subject, we want to write a little about *Hadith* and the book of *Imam Bukhari*.

HADITH

Hadith is the second fundamental source of *Shariah* in *Islam* and the *Ulama* (Scholars) unanimously declared those who do not believe it to be non-*Muslims*. The reason being is that believing so, would mean disbelief in the *Holy Quran*. The companions in writing and memory have preserved the *Ahadith* although they used to depend more upon memory. After the companions, the second generation (i.e. *Tabi'een*) received it from them, and they preserved that and so and so on. Even though all the *Ahadith* of the *Prophet* were written down from the very beginning in one way or the other, but still the *Umayyad Khalifa, Umar bin Abdul Aziz*, asked *Imam Zuhari*, a great *Imam* of *Hadith* and an authentic authority as well, to compile these *Ahadith*.

Now here is a misconception that *Ahadith* were written down in year 101 after *Hijrah*. This is wrong even in the time of the *Prophet*; some *Sahabah* used to write *Ahadith*. Details are there in our book *Science of Hadith*. Yes official compilation of *Ahadith* took place in year 101.

Later on, these great scholars, like *Imam Bukhari, Imam Muslim, Imam Abu Dawud*, and others, compiled their books. For their own compilations they adopted certain rules and criteria. For example, *Imam Bukhari* laid down a rule for himself that he would write a *Hadith* in his book, which is considered *Sahih* to his own research and approach.

Now it clearly means, that

(I)   Whatever he put in his book is *Sahih* according to his research; and

(II) That he has not put all *Sahih Ahadith* in his book, and that is why he said,

"*I chose these Ahadith from six hundred thousand Sahih Ahadith.*"

It means that neither all *Sahih Ahadith* are in his book, nor does it means that all *Ahadith* of *Bukhari* are *Sahih* to the research of other scholars. There are 80 narrators, about some of whom other scholars have reservations regarding their authenticity. Likewise, all *Ahadith* that *Imam Muslim* put in his book are to the level of *Sahih* according to his research, but other scholars have reservations about the 160 narrators of the book of *Imam Muslim*; that they are not to the level of *Sahih*.

Another point that is noteworthy is that the literal meaning of *Sahih* is correct or authentic, and the literal meaning of *Daeef* is weak, but in the science of *Hadith* these words have not been taken in its literal meaning, rather these are terms used by the scholars of this specific science.

As we know that the definition of the word terminology is

> *"The agreement of a group to put a word for a meaning."*

A *Sahih Hadith* to the scholars of *Hadith* is that *Hadith*, which is narrated by a narrator who is just and has perfect memory through a continuous chain, without any *Shuzooz* or *Illah*. So there are five conditions in the narration chain and narrators for a *Hadith* to be called *Sahih*.

Then, based upon those five previously mentioned conditions, other types of *Hadith* come about. For example, if the memory of a narrator is unreliable by around ten percent, then his *Hadith* is called *Hasan Lizatihi*. And if that is unreliable by thirty percent or more than his *Hadith* is called *Daeef*, but if the same *Daeef Hadith* is narrated by another narrator at the same stage of narration and with similar weak memory then because of two or more *Hadith* chains it elevates to the level of *Hasan Li Gharihi*. Also if the *Hadith* is based on these academic terms and is considered *Daeef*, it is still considered a *Hadith*. One cannot simply disregard it; there are more ways to analyze it and if the very text of the *Hadith* is not against certain things or it has been supported by the practice of the *Sahabah*, *Tabi'een*, logic, and reason, then that has been taken into consideration by the scholars. So for chain, there are five qualities to be taken into consideration, but for text there are fifteen or sixteen reasons to be considered in this regard.

As we know that there are two types of scholars:

(I) *MUHADITHEEN*

Muhaditheen who gathered together the *Ahadith,* and some of them compiled it.

(II) *FUQAHA*

Fuqaha (jurists), who deduced rules from the *Ahadith* and made it applicable.

A great *Muhaddith, Sulaiman Ibn Mehran Al-Aamash,* was asked about a few juristic issues. He asked *Imam Abu Hanifah* (a jurist) about them and when he answered these issues and also mentioned that with another issue, he had deduced from a *hadith.* While these *Ahadith*—mostly *Imam Abu Hanifah*—learned it from that great *Sheikh,* so *Sheikh* said

> "*O group of jurists! You are the doctors and we are the pharmacists.*"

Which means we have many *Ahadith* but we do not know how to apply them or how to deduce from them. The *Fuqaha* know this whole procedure. But these jurists were mostly involved with *Ahadith* relating to human life and they processed these *Ahadith* through great scrutiny of its chains and its texts as well.

SCRUTINY OF THE TEXT

The *Holy Quran* as a whole is *Mutawatir*, which means that it has been passed down from generation to generation by millions of people and therefore it does not need any further authentication, but in *Ahadith* narration there is a small number which is considered as *Mutawatir*. Yes sometimes, a *Hadith* is not *Mutawatir* in that sense a big number of *Sahabah*, *Tabi'een*, and later generations practiced it accordingly, so the scholars call it *Mutawatir Ul Amal*, practically *Mutawatir*. But most of the *Ahadith* are *Akhbari Ahad*, i.e. narrated by only one or two narrators and especially in the first and second stages, although later a big number narrated it. For *Khabari Wahid* the *Muhaditheen* scrutinize the chain, its continuity, and the narrators as well. They also scrutinize the text of the *Hadith*, so if there is a *Hadith*, then regarding its text they investigate that if it is:

(I)

NOT AGAINST THE TEXT OF *QURAN*

(II)

NOT AGAINST AN ESTABLISHED *SUNNAH*

(III)

NOT AGAINST THE CONSENSUS OF THE JURISTS

(IV)

NOT AGAINST SOMETHING WHICH IS PROVEN BY INTELLECT AND REASON ALREADY

(V)

NOT AGAINST A NATURALLY PROVEN THING

(VI)

NOT AGAINST HISTORICALLY PROVEN THING

(VII)

NOT AGAINST PROVEN NOBLE CHARACTER

(VIII)

NOT AGAINST SOMETHING PHYSICALLY AND/OR MEDICALLY PROVEN

(IX)

THE WORDS ARE NOT OF A NOBLE LEVEL

(X)

NOT AGAINST THE INTELLIGENT HABIT OF INTELLIGENT

PEOPLE

(XI)

IT DOES NOT CALL TOWARDS SUCH PRACTICE WHICH IS

AGAINST THE VERY NATURE OF *SHARIAH*

(XII)

IT IS NOT IN SUPPORT OF THE INNOVATION OF THE VERY

NARRATORS' FAITH

(XIII)

THE PRACTICE MENTIONED IN *HADITH* IS USUALLY DONE

IN PUBLIC BUT ONLY ONE PERSON NARRATES IT

(XIV)

A BIG REWARD IS MENTIONED FOR A VERY SMALL

ACTION IN THAT *HADITH*

(XV)

A TERRIBLE PUNISHMENT IS MENTIONED FOR A VERY SMALL SIN, AS THESE TWO DO NOT MAKE SENSE.

But as we mentioned that the *Fuqaha* were mainly involved with *Ahadith* related to worship, family rules, economics, and political systems, and that is why they did not talk that much about *Ahadith* like the one regarding the age of *Aaisha* at the time of her marriage, but they laid down certain rules to accept a *Hadith* or to reject it, to take into consideration or to put it aside.

Likewise, the *Muhaditheen* also put certain rules for the authentication of *Ahadith*. Some of these rules are agreed upon, while others differ from *Muhaddith* to *Muhaddith* like *Hadith Mu'an'an*, where a narrator used the word *"un"* which means *"from"*, to indicate that he narrates from another source. The narrator did not use the word *Haddathana* or *Akhbarana*, which clearly expresses that he has taken it from another *Sheikh* directly, while the word *"un"* does not express this clearly, meaning it may be or may not be.

Imam Muslim says that if the narrator is not known for hiding the name of his own teacher and referring to someone more famous and authentic than his own teacher and he and the one whom he narrated it from lived in the same time, in such a way that there was a possibility of meeting each other, then that *Hadith* is *Muttasil* and if all other required qualities were found in that *Hadith* then that will be *Sahih* also. On the other hand, *Imam Bukhari* in such a case says that actual meeting of both must be proven once or twice, then it will be considered *Muttasil*. This is also worthy of mention that finding out the status of a *Hadith* is a matter of research, so there can be a *Hadith* which is proven *Sahih* according to the research of all *Muhaditheen*. Conversely, there can be a *Hadith* which is proven *Sahih* to some, but is *Daeef* to others. So whenever we say this *Hadith* is *Daeef* or *Sahih*, we must find out whether this is according to all the *Muhaditheen* or whether they have different approaches in this regard. This is one of the reasons that the jurists differ with each other in rulings. Also, they look into the *Ahadith*: if two separate *Ahadith* differ from each other in a specific issue, then they are trying to do a patch-up of both. If there is no way to do this, then they consider the issue concerned. For example, on an issue that relates to women, where one *Hadith* is related by a male *Sahabi* and the other by a female, they prefer the narration by the female.

IMAM BUKHARI AND *SAHIH*

BUKHARI

Due to the tough scrutiny of *Ahadith* by *Imam Bukhari*, the majority of *ulama* (scholars) said that the much more authentic book after the book of *Allah* is *Sahih Bukhari*. Even though some of the scholars like *Imam Hakim* said so far it is the book of *Imam Muslim*, and some others said the same regarding the *Mu'atta* of *Imam Malik*. But still they are the efforts of a human even though he was a great man.

Imam Bukhari started compiling his book at the age of eighteen until old age. The book of *Imam Bukhari* has been narrated by many people, but the famous narration is that of the book written by *Mohammad Ibn Yusuf Al Firabri (320 A.H.)*, but there are others, like the book by

(I) *IBRAHIM IBN MAQIL AN NASAFI (294 A.H.)*,

(II) *HAMMAD IBN SHAKIR AN NASAFI (311 A.H.)*, and

(III) _ABU TALHA MANSOOR IBN MOHAMMAD_ _(329 A.H.) (FATHUL BARI)._

In the book of _Firabri_ there are 200 more _Ahadith_ than the book of _Hammad_, and 300 more than the book of _Ibrahim_. This is because _Firabri_ is the student of _Imam Bukhari_ who narrated this at the later portion of _Imam Bukhari's_ life.

This reveals that _Imam Bukhari_ was trying to make his book as perfect as he can until the end of his life. Even though _Imam Bukhari_, wherever he has narrated a _Hadith_ as a _Taaleeq_ (lacking a narration chain) he either mentioned the same along with its chain, somewhere else in his book or this is a known fact that he made himself bound to put, only a _Muttasil Hadith_ in his book, so that is _Muttasil_.

Before we scrutinize the relevant _Hadith_, we want to mention certain events about the birth and age of _Aaisha_:

THE BIRTH AND AGE OF *AAISHA*

1.

TABARI

Tabari the historian relates that *Abu Bakr* married *Qateelah Bint Abdul Uzza* in the time of ignorance and begot from her a son named *Abdullah* and a daughter named *Asma*. Then he married *Ummi Roman Bint Aamir* and from her he begot *Abdur Rahman* and *Aaisha*. Then he said,

> *"These four whom I named from these two ladies were born in the time of ignorance."*

2.

IBN ISHAQ AND *IBN HISHAM*

The two ancient historians and writers of *Seerat un Nabi*, *Ibn Ishaq* and *Ibn Hisham*, both mentioned *Aaisha* in the list of *As Sabiqoonal Awwaloon*, the first forerunners in *Islam*. They accepted *Islam* in the first three years of the message when the *Prophet* was giving the call secretly. *Ibn Hisham* mentioned *Aaisha* on the list and noted that she was a minor.

Hafiz Ibn Kathir has put her name on as number eighteen of these forerunners (*As Seerat Un Nabawiyyah*). Her name is also mentioned in the list in *Ar Rosul Anf* by *Muhaddith Abdur Rahman*. It means that she was a minor but mature, at least of six or seven years, because they mentioned her older sister *Asma* in this list and she is noted as having attained puberty, i.e., sixteen or seventeen years of age, and she was older than *Aaisha* by ten years, as *Khatib* and others have said. Historian *Ibn Ishaq* mentioned the name of *Aaisha* as the twentieth forerunner in *Islam*. *Zurqani*, *Ibn Hisham*, and *Ibn Hajar* mentioned *Aaisha* in the list of fifty forerunners in *Islam*.

3.

HAFIZ IBN HAJAR

Hafiz Ibn Hajar said that *Fatima* was older than *Aaisha* by five years (*Al Isabah*) and as we mentioned, *Abbas* told *Fatima*,

> *"You were born the year Quraish reconstructed the Kaaba."*

This reconstruction was five years before the message. Keeping in view, this narration also states that *Aaisha* was born in the first year of the message, so she should be fifteen or more at the time of her marriage.

4.

IMAM BUKHARI

Imam Bukhari narrated from *Abu Hurairah* that in year 3 after the message when *Allah* said

"And warn your kin (relatives) (26:214)",

The *Prophet* of *Allah* gathered them together and warned them by name of the tribe. That *O Bani Abdi Manaf*, then some of them by name and in these names he mentioned *Fatima* by name.

If *Fatima* were not mature at that time, then why would he address a baby girl?

This means that at least she was born six or seven years before the message. So her age at the time of this address would have been nine or ten, and *Aaisha*, who was younger than *Fatima* by five years, would have been of four or five years of age.

5.

IMAM BUKHARI

Related from *Ibn Masud* that in the fourth or fifth year after Prophethood, the *Prophet* was praying in the vicinity of the *Kaaba* and when he was in *Sajdah*, *Oqbah Ibn Abi Mo'eet* brought the fetus of a camel full of filth, and put it on the back of the *Prophet*. Due to this the *Prophet* couldn't lift his head, so *Fatima* came and she threw it off the *Prophet's* back. It means that she was big enough to lift at least 20 to 30 kg, depending on how big and advanced the fetus was. So her age would be ten or eleven at that time, so again *Aaisha* would have been six years old at that time. In the 2nd year after *Hijrah* at the time of her marriage, she would have been seventeen or eighteen years old.

6.

FATIMA

When the *Prophet* passed away, *Fatima* was twenty-nine or thirty years. When *Hisham Ibn Abdul Malik* (The Caliph) asked *Abdullah Ibn Hasan* about the age of *Fatima* at the time of her death, he said she was thirty (*Zubair Ibn Bakkar*). The *Prophet* passed away in *Rabeeul Awwal*, 11th year after *Hijrah*, and *Fatima* passed away the same year in the month of *Ramadan*. So the age of *Aaisha* at the time of the passing of the *Prophet* would have been twenty-six or more. So in 2nd year after *Hijrah*, she would have been seventeen or eighteen years old.

7.

OSAMAH IBN ZAID

Osamah Ibn Zaid, who is called the beloved of the *Prophet*, was nineteen or twenty at the time of the *Prophet's* death, as he was appointed as a leading general of the army to go to *Sham*. Nineteen is mentioned by *Khatib Al Baghdadi* and twenty by *Hafiz Ibn Kathir*. *Ibn Majah and Ibn Sa'd* narrated from *Aaisha* that the *Prophet* came to the house of *Abu Bakr* along with *Osamah*.

> *"Osamah fell down on the threshold and was injured,
> the Prophet said to me to clean his face, but his nose
> was running and I disliked it, then the Prophet himself
> stood up and cleaned his nose and said, 'Aaisha! Love
> him, as I love him (Tirmidhi)."*

Osamah was born in the third year after Prophethood and when he came with the *Prophet* to the house of *Abu Bakr* walking on his own, so he must have been at least six or seven years old. This case happened in the tenth year after Prophethood, and *Aaisha* was certainly bigger than him, which is why the *Prophet* told her to clean his face. So at the time she would have been of thirteen or fourteen years old, therefore at the time of her marriage she would have been eighteen or nineteen years in the second year after *Hijrah*.

8.

IMAM BUKHARI

Imam Bukhari related that the *Prophet* sent *Aaisha* to inquire about the health and nurse *Abu Bakr, Aamir Ibn Fuhairah*, and *Bilal*, who fell sick when they came to *Medina*. When she came back she narrated their situation and also narrated the poetry they were singing in that situation (*Bukhari, Ibn Sa'd, Ahmad*).

This means she was very mature at that time, i.e. before her marriage in the second year after *Hijrah*, due to her nursing them and also that she was able to memorize what they were singing.

9.

THE *BATTLE OF UHUD*

The *Battle of Uhud* took place in the 3rd year after *Hijrah*. *Umm Sulaim* and *Aaisha* were bringing water in skin bags for the injured, so if she was only nine in the second year, then at this time she was only ten years old, and the *Prophet* was not even allowing boys that young to go to the battle field, so how could the girls of such a small age be there?

Also such a young girl would not have been able to carry a full skin of water, so she must have been over sixteen.

10.

THE *BATTLE OF BADR*

In the *Battle of Badr* the *Prophet* made a flag out of *Aaisha's* shawl, which means she was there and when some cloth was needed for a flag, she offered her shawl. It does not make sense that the *Prophet* would take her cloak with him to make a flag later. This means she was there and as a known rule she was over fifteen years of age.

11.

IMAM MUSLIM

It is known from a narration of *Imam Muslim* that she was there in *Badr* as she narrates that one man came to the *Prophet* in *Bahratul Ghareerah* and then in *Shajarah* asking to join the *Battle of Badr*, but the *Prophet* did not accept him, as he was not *Muslim*. Then he came in *Baida* once again and accepted *Islam*, and the *Prophet* allowed him. The context of the narration and its narrative clearly shows that she was there, which means that she was older than fifteen.

12.

HADITH OF *BUKHARI* AND *MUSLIM*

It is known from a *Hadith* of *Bukhari* and *Muslim* that *Aaisha* joined *Badr* and *Uhud*. When *Umar* fixed some special or extra stipend for those who attended *Badr*, *Aaisha* was also receiving the same amount (*Muslim*). It means she took part in *Badr*.

13.

KHATIB'S AL IKMAL THAT *ASMA*

Khatib has written in *Al Ikmal* that *Asma*, the sister of *Aaisha*, was ten years older than *Aaisha*. She was the wife of *Zubair* and the mother of *Abdullah Ibn Zubair*. She passed away 73 years after *Hijrah*, at the age of 100 after the crucifixion of her son *Abdullah* in *Makkah*. At the time of *Hijrah* her age was twenty-seven, so *Aaisha* was seventeen years old. This ten-year age difference between *Asma* and *Aaisha* is mentioned by *Hafiz Ibn Kathir* in *Al Bidayah*, by *Zahabi* in *"Sear"*, by *Ibn Asakir* and by *Bayhaqi* in *As Sunan*, and *Ibn Hajar* in *Taqreeb*. So at the time of the marriage, the age of *Aaisha* must have been eighteen or nineteen.

14.

IMAM BUKHARI

Imam Bukhari related from *Aaisha* that *Surah Qamar*, verse number 46, was revealed and at that time I was a girl playing. Now *Surah Qamar* was revealed in the fifth year of Prophethood. This is also said that the aforementioned verse was revealed in the 8th year after Prophethood, because the moon cleft asunder around five years before *Hijrah*, which means in the 8th year of Prophethood she was a mature girl and that is why she called herself *Jariyah*, which means *"girl."*

15.

KHADIJAH

Khadijah passed away in 10ᵗʰ year of Prophethood. *Uthman Ibn Maz'oon* was the fostering brother of the *Prophet*. His wife *Khaulah Bint Hakeem* said to the *Prophet*,

"You should now re-marry,"

And she also mentioned *Saudah* and *Aaisha* as potential brides. The *Prophet* sent her to women, but as *Aaisha* was engaged to *Jubair Ibn Mut'im*, *Abu Bakr* said,

"Let us see what he thinks,"

And *Abu Bakr* spoke to *Mut'im Ibn Adi*. They were not ready yet so *Abu Bakr* said,

"Let me have her engaged to the Prophet."

This means that in the 10ᵗʰ year after Prophethood, *Aaisha* was at least fourteen or fifteen years old, otherwise the narration of *Hisham Ibn Urwah* from *Urwah* means that she was born in the sixth or seventh year of Prophethood.

So *Abu Bakr* was asking *Mut'im* to take a girl of four or five years old as his son's bride?

Actually, her engagement to *Jubair* had taken place before *Hijrah* to *Habashah*, which took place in the 5ᵗʰ year. And as we know that *Jubair* was one of those people who were named by the *Makkans* to kill the *Prophet*, meaning that he was a healthy young man.

So how is it possible that he had become engaged a baby girl of two or three years?

Also *Abu Bakr* did not say to *Khaulah* that it was all right to do such a thing. *Aaisha* was still a baby and the *Prophet* needs a mature lady to get married. Then *Abu Bakr* waited for *Mut'im's* family to have the final word, and they gave it in the 13th year of Prophethood. This idea gets support from the saying of *Aaisha*,

> "I never became jealous of any women, like that of Khadijah even though she passed away three years before my Nikah."

It is also known that *Khadijah* passed in the tenth year of Prophethood. The *Prophet* got engaged then in the second year after *Hijrah*. *Aaisha* was a woman of more than nineteen years, as *Bukhari* narrated from *Amrah Binti Abdur Rahman* that *Aaisha* told me that after some time in *Madinah*, that *Abu Bakr* asked the *Prophet*,

> "How will you take Aaisha as your wife to your house?"

The *Prophet* said,

> "The only excuse is the Mahr [bride-price]."

Then *Abu Bakr* gave him about 500 *Dirhams*, which the *Prophet* gave him as *Mahr*. It means she was then a mature woman, otherwise the *Prophet* would have said that she was still too young.

16.

As we mentioned before, disbelievers and hypocrites used to look for some loophole to make a scene against the *Prophet* and to propagate against him. So if *Aaisha* was only nine and the *Prophet* married her, would they have kept quiet? Not at all. They would have taken the issue to its utmost against him.

We have established that before the age of puberty, *Nikah* is not recommended, and if a girl tried to secure one by herself, then it would be void. If a guardian other than a father and grandfather did that, it would be settled, but she has the right, after attaining puberty, to ask for an annulment. And if her father or grandfather had done it, it would normally be based upon affection, as it is natural that fathers and grandfathers are very affectionate toward their children, but if it is looks otherwise, then again, she has that right to dissolve it. The reason for this is that each type of guardianship is based upon advantage, so if something is otherwise, then it may be undone. But consummation must be after puberty, as a minor is not *Mukallaf*, i.e. bound by the rules of *Shariah*.

QAZI IBN SHUBRUMAH

Qazi Ibn Shubrumah said that marriage is all right for boys of eighteen and girls of sixteen. The same is the juristic opinion of *Abu Bakr*; *Abu Bakral Asam* and *Imam Sarakhsi* said that for both, marriage before this age is not appropriate. And *Abu Bakr Al Jassas* said that even though if their fathers would do their *Nikah* before this age, so to these two great Jurists, that *Nikah* is not done (*Al Mabsut, Ahkam Al Quran*).

56

As we mentioned before, the *Prophet* was a role model in each and every aspect of human life, and that is why his every word and action is preserved in the best way. The scholars imposed very strict rules to keep his words intact and to protect them from any fabrication, perversion, or misconception. In this regard and for the said purpose, they not only preserved 750,000 *Ahadith* of the *Prophet*, but they also preserved the biography of almost 500,000 narrators of different times and ages. They also mentioned the position of every narrator and the status of every *Hadith*.

SCRUTINY OF THE *HADITH*

Regarding *Hadith* in general, we have already mentioned a few important points, and as we said, for the *Muhaditheen* to put a *Hadith* in their book or to quote it, they must do research and note its status, and the jurists also apply a *Hadith* and look into its research, but they also look into the matter to which the *Hadith* is related, and if there is something in the narration chain such as a disconnection, then they look into the treasury of *Hadith* if the same subject is narrated there through another connected chain. Then they investigate the status of the narrators, of what the critics said about them, and then they investigate the treasury to see if there is any other *Hadith* that relates a contradicting concept. Then, if one of these two *Ahadith* is higher in position then the other, they give priority to the higher one if no patch-up is possible.

It is true that for priority there are certain rules they agree upon but there are rules that differ from one another, and they consider this in case of two contradicting *Ahadith* when they are of the same status and level.

For example, *Imam Shafi* said that a *Hadith* narrated by a *Sahabi* who has a big treasury of narration takes precedence over the narrations of the other. And *Imam Abu Hanifah* said that if the issue is

Fiqhi (juristic) then the narration of a greater jurist *Sahabi* is prior to the narration of one who is not of that level, or if one of them only narrates and the other one says,

"I was there,"

Or the issue is related to him, or, for example, that issue is related to women, and a female *Sahabiyah* is relating it. Or if the case is that of the *Prophet's* house, and one of the wives of the *Prophet* related it, then this is sufficient reason for its priority, and if there is no similar thing then they try if they can find any proof of different times to call one of these two as abrogated.

ISSUES WHICH DEGRADE A *HADITH'S* LEVEL

1. *TADLEES* - OR MISQUOTING THE NARRATORS.

We already mentioned this, but only briefly. It means that some-time a narrator narrates a *Hadith* with word *un*, which means that this narrator has heard it from this teacher he mentioned or he dropped his teacher and quoted someone more famous and authentic than he, so if this narrator is known for this practice in a wrong way then his *Hadith* is a type of *Munqati*, i.e. disconnected. But if he himself is authentic and does not do wrong, then *Imam Muslim* says that in case of the possibility of their meeting it is considered as *Muttasil* (connected), while *Imam Bukhari* says for its connection their meeting once or twice must be proven. *Tadlees* in its basic sense is *Haram* in narration like *Zina* in character and society.

2. *TALFEEQ* -

The conjoining of two events with one another in such a way that it appears as if they happened at the same time, meaning that they drop the time gap.

3. *IDRAJ* (INSERTION/ ANNOTATION) -

As in the narrative the narrator put some words from his side, which appear to be those of the *Prophet*. Sometimes that is in a good sense, as he explains a strange word with a known one, but he explains it that is

"From me or my sheikh (teachers)."

4. *ISTINTAJ* (INFERENCE)

When a narrator gets an idea from the *Hadith*, he narrates and mentions it in the narration so that later it looks like the part of *Hadith*.

SORTING RULES

As we said, for *Ahadith* to sort out its level and status the scholars (critics) laid down rules in 180 after *Hijrah* and the *Hadith* of *Urwah* came on the scene 185 years after *Hijrah*, and it spread in 220 after *Hijrah*, so regarding this *Hadith* of marriage these rules were not considered because of many reasons.

(1)

THE HADITH IS NARRATED WITH WORD *UN*

This *Hadith* is narrated with word *Un*, which carries the possibility that the narrator has not heard it from the teacher he narrates from.

(2)

URWAH, *ABU SALAMAH*, *ASWAD*, AND *ABU OBAIDAH*

Urwah, *Abu Salamah*, *Aswad*, and *Abu Obaidah*, who narrated it never heard it from *Aaisha* collectively, i.e. together, as two of them are from *Kufa* and their traveling to *Madinah* is not proven anywhere. That is why *Imam Bukhari* narrated only the narration of *Urwah*, but he did not put the narration of these others even as *Mutabi* (support), and *Imam Tirmizi* has not narrated this either.

(3)

ABU SALAMAH

In the narration of *Abu Salamah*, the first form and third form are used. The narrator said of the *Prophet*, that he betrothed *Aaisha* when she was six; while this is also said,

"The Prophet betrothed me when I was six."

This change of form makes doubt that who said this number of six years.

(4)

ZUHARI

This *Hadith* is not narrated from *Zuhari* from *Urwah*, but only by *Imam Muslim*, while it is not proven that *Zuhari* ever heard from *Ur-wah*. So his name has been put for authenticity and *Zuhari* passed away 61 years before this *Hadith* appeared. So this could either be *Tadleesi Badal* that the name of some other narrator is changed to Zuhari or *Tadleesi Qata* to give authenticity to it by this great name.

The chain of narration of *Zuhari* is *Abd ibn Humaid*, from *Abdur Razzaq*, from *Mamar*, from *Zuhari*, from *Urwah*. *Zuhari* had hundreds of students, but only *Mamar* narrates it from *Zuhari and* only, *Abdur Razzaq* narrated it from him, and from him only *Abd Ibn Humaid*, while all of them had thousands of students, and they have not narrated it.

(5)

ABU BAKR

No one from the family of *Abu Bakr* has narrated this age issue, only *Hisham* from his father *Urwah*, and we will discuss him later.

(6)

ABU HURAIRAH, IBN ABBAS, JABIR, ABU SAEED AL KHUDRI, IBN UMAR

Abu Hurairah, Ibn Abbas, Jabir, Abu Saeed Al Khudri, Ibn Umar are considered the big narrators, but they have not narrated this issue, Not even the wives of the *Prophet* or other family members like *Zaid Ibn Haritha*, his son *Osamah*, his wife *Umm Aiman*, who was the first fostering mother of *Prophet*, or *Bareera*, the servant girl of *Aaisha*, have narrated it. Neither has *Anas* narrated it, and he served the *Prophet* for ten years, and lived to be almost 100. *Abdullah Ibn Zubair*, the big brother of *Urwah*, has not narrated this since his mother, *Asma*, is the big sister of *Aaisha*.

(7)

Up to 230 years after *Hijrah*, the great *Muhaditheen* like *Abu Hanifah, Malik, Muhammad,* and the great historians like *Ibn Ishaq, Ibn Hisham, Ibn Sa'd, Abu Dawud, At Tayalisi,* have not narrated this *Hadith.*

(8)

KUFA OR FROM *BASRAH*

The first narrators of this *Hadith* are either from *Kufa* or from *Basrah,* and since the time of the battle of *Jamal* between *Ali* and *Aaisha,* the ideas in those two cities about *Aaisha* is well known even the same *Sunnis* there got some influence of the *Tashayyu (Shiite)* in some concepts even *Sheikh Abdur Razzaq* the great, *Muhaddith,* is accused of *Shiite* tendencies by some scholars due to his inclination to *Ahle-Bait* and *Imam Aamash* is blamed that he is prejudice towards *Aaisha.*

(9)

URWAH

Urwah is a big name. He is the treasurer of the knowledge of *Aaisha,* his aunt. But his son *Hisham* was born in year 61 after *Hijrah.* He never related this *Hadith* from his father in his stay at *Madinah* for 71 years, but when he came to Iraq he was blind and senile. His mind was not whole at the time he narrated this *Hadith* in 145 after *Hijrah.* This *Hadith* came on the scene in 185 after *Hijrah* for the first time by a student of *Hisham* named *Ali Ibn Mis'har Al Kufi,* almost 39 years after the death of *Hisham,* and this was ten years before the birth of *Imam Bukhari*. He was born in 195 after *Hijrah* and passed away in 256 after *Hijrah*. *Imam Bukhari* would have received this *Hadith* at least in year 215, as he travelled to *Kufa* in 212 for the first time. It would have been the case of *Imam Darimi* and *Ibn Majah* as well, as they put it in their books after year 250.

(10)

ABU DAWUD, BAYHAQI, AND SHAFI

In other books like *Abu Dawud*, *Bayhaqi*, and *Shafi* in *Kitab Al Umm* narrated this through the chain to *Hisham* to *Urwah*. In *Muslim Sharif* its other narrators besides *Hisham* are *Zuhari* and *Aswad*. In *Nasa'i* there are these two and *Abu Salamah*. In addition to *Hisham* in *Ibn Majah* there is *Abu Obaidah*. In *Musnad* of *Imam Ahmad* there are *Aswad* and *Abu Salamah* besides *Hisham*. And the two mentioned, their travel to *Madinah* is not proven, and they are *Kufis*. About *Zuhari*, we said his hearing is not proven from *Urwah* (*Ibn Hajar, Ibn Abi Hatam, Tahawi*).

ABU OBAIDAH

The narration of *Abu Obaidah* has four narrators: *Qutaibah, Abthar, Muttarif,* and *Abu Ishaq*. This *Qutaibah* narrated a *Hadith* of praying two prayers at once from *Laith* while *Laith* died in 171 after *Hijrah*, and *Qutaibah* was a minor. Therefore, *Hakim* said this is fake (*Tahzeeb*).

ABU ISHAQ

The narration of *Abu Ishaq*:

Abu Ishaq is from *Kufa*. His name is *Amr Ibn Abdullah*, and he narrates from *Ali* and *Mughirah Ibn Shobah*, but his hearing from them both is not proven. He also narrates from *Abdullah Ibn Masud* while he and *Abdullah's* son, *Abu Obaidah* were of the same age and they both did not hear from *Abdullah*. He put *Abu Obaidah's* name for authentication, *Abu Ishaq* was also influenced by *Shie'ee* concepts.

ABU SALAMAH

The narration of *Abu Salamah*:

This is from *Saeed Ibn Hakam*, from *Yahya Ibn Ayub*, from *Ammar Ibn Ghaziyah*, from *Muhammad Ibn Ibrahim*, from *Abu Salamah* from *Aaisha*. The first three narrators are from *Egypt* and the critics did not consider them, as *Saeed* was narrating with a wrong chain (*Tahzeeb*). While *Yahya* memory was not good as *Ahmad* said (*Tahzeeb*), and *Ammar* is *Daeef* according to *Ibn Hazm* and *Aqeeli*. Also all these narrations came to the front when *Hisham's* narration appeared.

WHO IS *HISHAM*?

He was the son of *Urwah Ibn Zubair*. *Urwah's* mother was *Asma Bint Abu Bakr*, the *Aaisha's* older sister. He was an authentic narrator as long as he was ok and stayed in *Madinah* for almost seventy-one years. So many authentic people took *hadith* from him, including *Imam Malik*. He later on left *Madinah* due to lot of debts and went to

Baghdad and became blind and lost his memory. In *Meezanul Itidaal*, it is said that he related certain things he could not express properly. For example, he said once that

> "*my wife was thirteen years older than me and she was nine years old when I married her (Tahzeeb).*"

Hafiz Zahabi said her age was twenty-nine at the time of marriage, but he expressed that as nine. We say that like that he expressed the age of *Aaisha* at six years of age at the time of engagement and nine at the time of marriage, instead of sixteen and nineteen. As in *Arabic* for six the word is *Sitta* and for sixteen it is *Sitta Ashara*, so he apparently left off *Ashara*. And for nine it is *Tis'aa* and for nineteen it is *Tis'aa Shara*, so again he dropped *Ashara*.

Imam Malik and other scholars from *Madinah* did not accept the *Ahadith* that he narrated in *Iraq* (*Tahzeeb*).

Hafiz Zahabi said that in *Iraq*, when he lost his memory he was relating from his father *Ahadith* that he had not taken from his father (*Al-Itidaal*).

He travelled to *Iraq* three times. It became his habit that whatever *Hadith* he was relating he attributed it to his father, even though he had taken it from somebody else, and that is why *Imam Malik* called him a liar. He was mixing *Ahadith* a lot in that age. It is also possible that he did not say this; maybe somebody else put it in his name.

Also this is amazing that not only he, but *Ali Ibn Mis'har*, *Abu Mua'wiyah* and *Dareer*, all these narrators of this *Hadith* became blind in their old age and it is a rule that in the case of blindness, *Hadith* narrated from memory is not accepted.

If a narrator was healthy before in accordance with the qualities and conditions the *Muhaditheen* mentioned, his narration of that time is reliable but in old age when he lost his memory, then the case is different. This is the case with *Hisham*, some other *Ahadith* in which it is said that *Aaisha* used to play with her dolls, it is either looking for inference of narrators as she was the only virgin among the wives of the *Prophet*. Also it could be conjoining of events sometime back when she was playing with dolls, some narrators linked it to her marriage. Also to play with dolls is not unheard of among mature women; for example, when a woman does not have children, she may do that.

Based on all these details it became clear that at the time of betrothal *Aaisha* was sixteen or seventeen and at the time of her marriage she was eighteen or nineteen. *Aaisha* died in the year 58 after *Hijrah* while *Mua'wiyah* was *Caliph*, and her age was seventy-six. She lived as a widow for forty-seven years, which means at the time of the death of the *Prophet* she was twenty-seven years old. The *Prophet* died in year 11 after *Hijrah*, so in the second year after *Hijrah* her age was eighteen or nineteen.

IMPORTANT POINT

Instead of the age issue, the rule in *Shariah* is that consummation of marriage is allowed after the girl has attained the age of puberty, and *Aaisha* had reached the age of puberty by that time of her marriage. That is why *Khaulah Bint Hakim* mentioned her to the *Prophet* as *Bakirah* which means a virgin, and this word is also used for a girl who has attained puberty.

Islamic Shariah, as we said does not validate or allow the *Nikah* of a girl before puberty if she initiates it herself. Also, if a guardian other than her father and grandfather initiates it, then she has the right to ask for dissolution when she attains puberty, and if her father or grandfather initiates it out of affection and compassion for their children naturally, then that is acceptable according to *Imam Abu Hanifah*. But if it is seen that there is no affection then after puberty and before consummation, she can ask for dissolution, but *Ibn Shubrumah* and *Abu Bakr Al Asam* both are of the view that it is not acceptable even if the father or grandfather has done it. It is also looks like *Imam Jassas* from the *Hanafites* is also from the same view, the way he mentioned their opinion in *Ahkam Ul Quran* and *Sarakhsi* also mentioned in *Al Mabsut*. As far as consummation of marriage is concerned, it is not allowed with a minor who has not reached puberty, as this is abusive and unnatural. *Islam* is *Deen Ul Fitrah*, a *Deen* of nature or a natural *Deen*. And those who allowed the *Nikah* of a minor also said that she has the right to object to it if it is done by a guardian other than her father or grandfather when she attains puberty. They also said if the marriage is consummated (after she attains puberty) then her marriage is indissoluble. In the case of consummation before puberty, it is a contradiction after attaining puberty whether she can exercise the right or not, because upon reaching puberty she can do that, but once the marriage is consummated then she cannot exercise her right to dissolve the marriage. How can we deprive someone of her right because of an action when she was a minor, as at the time she was not *Mukallaf*, or bound by *Shariah* law?

> *"And test the orphan until they arrive at the age of Ni-*
> *kah, then if you saw of them manhood then give them*
> *their wealth (4:6)."*

This verse is also a support, but even a base of the idea that *Nikah* must be after the age of puberty, as *Allah* referred to puberty and used the word *Nikah*, as no one says that a minor should be given their wealth. The only thing is that we can say this word *Nikah* is used in reference to consummation, so only betrothal could be allowed before puberty, as we discussed.

Looking after wealth of an orphan (who is by nature a child, as there is no state of orphanage after puberty) is as important than taking care of his health and body, and ensuring that there is no abuse is very important, especially for girls.

Verse number 4 chapter 65 said,

"And those of your women who have passed the age of monthly courses for them the Iddat [waiting period] if you doubt [about their menses] is three months and for those [also] who have no courses (65:4)."

As for the last part of the verse,

"Those who have no courses,"

some scholars said its implies that consummation is acceptable if one has not reached puberty. But we say that if this would have been the case then *Allah* would have said *Lamma Yahidna*, meaning a girl whose menses has not come yet, but he said, *Lum Yahidna* which means whose menses do not come when it should. In other words, due to some physical or medical issue, they do not menstruate even though they are old enough to do so. Despite what some scholars said, we say that in this verse *Allah* is telling us the rule about *Iddat*: that if it happened and a marriage with a minor girl is consummated then *Iddat* is three months, but it does not mean that consummation with a minor is allowed. Like we say if someone commits *Zina* (illegitimate sex), then taking a shower is *Fard* (necessary) but we cannot say that it means *Zina* is allowed, just because *Shariah* has made rules about what must come after it if it is committed.

These details does not degrade or lessen the high status of the book of *Bukhari* or *Muslim*, because in *Ahadith* and its sciences there is one thing called *Tas'heef*, what we might call a misprint nowadays, that may be this is a misprint as we said of *Sitta* and *Sitta Ashara* and *Tis'aa* and *Tis'aa Ashara* that the word *Ashara* is dropped, either due to the speaking weakness of *Hisham* in his dotage or it is not written

72

even though he has said it or sometimes the talk is going on and some-thing is already spoken and the person concerned is adding to it so *Ashara* was mentioned and *Hisham* said *Sitta* and *Tis'aa* means added to that *Ashara*.

In brief, we say that *Islam* allows consummation at the age of puberty and *Aaisha* was at the age of puberty, and a virgin, at nineteen years of age. This issue about the last and final *Prophet* of *Allah* is hotly debated, and we as *Muslims* are bound to give the utmost respect and to defend and protect his personality, as he is the nucleus of our faith.

Allah said:

> *"Then those who believed in him honor [magnify] him, help him, and followed the light which has been sent down with him they are the successful people (7:157)."*

Also *Allah* said:

> *"Indeed we have sent you a witness [teacher], a giver of glad tidings, a warner, in order that you people may believe in Allah, in His Messenger, and to assist him, to honor him and to glorify Allah in morning and in the afternoon (48:8-9)."*

Also He said:

"Indeed Allah and his angels send graces on the Prophet, O you who believe send graces on him and protect him perfectly (33:56)."

And He said:

"Verily those who annoy Allah and his Messenger, Allah has curse them in this world and in the hereafter and has prepared for them a humiliating torment (33:57)."

May *Allah* accept this effort for his good pleasure and the good pleasure of his *Prophet* and may *Allah* make it a good treatment for hearts full of sickness. *Aamin.*

BOOKS BY *QAZI FAZL ULLAH*

Qazi Fazl Ullah has written other books. Below is a brief list with summaries.

FIQH KEE TAREEKH WA IRTIQA (URDU)

Islam is *Deen* (religion) and is a complete code of life. Its laws are of two types, textual and deduced, but how the text is interpreted and how laws are deduced therefrom is called *"Jurisprudence"* and the laws are called *Fiqh,* and how this *Fiqh* got developed and compiled. This book gives the details about its stages of development.

MOHAMMADUR RASOOLULLAH (URDU)

The biography of the *Prophet Mohammad* was preserved from day one by his blessed companions. Then scholars and historians have written books in this regard in various times, both concise and detailed. This book on the biography of *Prophet Mohammad* is an excellent balance of concise and detailed, as a concise a book sometimes misses things, and people do not have time to read and understand too detailed a book. Another important feature of this book is that almost with every important part of the *Prophet's* biography, the relevant part of the *Holy Quran* has been quoted, which illustrates that the *Prophet's* life was the practical shape of the *Holy Book*.

SARMAYA DARANA NIZAM ISHTIRAKIYAT AUR ISLAM (URDU)

Humans, throughout their history, have thought ahead and planned their economics and economical needs. They created systems for these purposes. The three systems most widely practiced in history are capitalism, communism, and *Islam*. This book is a comparative study of these 3 economical systems, and it proves that the *Islamic* system bestowed upon us by the Creator is the best one with regard to justice and no room for exploitation.

DAWAT O JIHAD (URDU)

The basic duty of every *Prophet* and his followers was and is to call the people towards *Allah* in a peaceful, attractive, and convincing way, and wherever and whenever they encounter resistance and hindrances in this regard, they must remove these hindrances. At times, this leads to fights, as when the conspiracy is big and the opponents try to take away their fundamental rights, so they have the right to defend it but how, when, and where? In this book, it is mentioned that *Islam* teaches us to convey, convince, and convert, but not to coerce. This book is an answer to anti-*Islamic* propaganda, especially about the concept of *Jihad* in *Islam*.

ISLAM AUR SIYASAT (URDU)

Islam and Politics—as it is known from the title that this book discusses *Islamic* political system, because *Islam* is *Deen*, meaning a complete code of life and not a set of a few rituals. It has its own system for state and government. So, wherever *Muslims* are in power, if they will implement this system, they meet the needs of everyone, regardless of color, caste, or religion. *Islam* covers the details, such as how to elect a government, and how to run the state to provide peace and justice to all.

RIYASATI ISLAMI KA TASWWAR (URDU)

The title means the concept of an *Islamic* state, and *"concept"* means its conduct. In this book, it is mentioned how and why a state and government is needed, and how that state and government may be and should be run. The Creator *Allah* the Almighty knows all our needs, necessities, qualities, and shortcomings, so the system he has given is the only system that can ensure people's security and safety and can provide them peace and justice, making the state a welfare state.

USOOLUT - TAFSEER (ARABIC)

Every branch of science has its own rules, principles, and methodologies, which provide guidelines for explaining it and how to interpret it, so this methodology is a circle or limits one may keep himself confines to, so he will not get lost or go astray.

This book covers the explanation of the *Holy Quran*, the last and final book of *Allah*. The book of *Allah* is the basic source of *Islam* and *Islamic* law, so its explanation requires certain rules to be followed in its explanation, so one may not be unbridled and without restraint, otherwise he will put his faith in danger.

DIRAYATUR RIWAYAH (ARABIC)

Hadith (sayings, actions, and sanctions) of *Prophet Mohammad* is the second fundamental source of *Islam* and *Islamic* laws and also it is the interpretation of the *Holy Quran*. The companions of the *Prophet Mohammad* have preserved them in their memories and in their scriptures and the second and third generation took it from them and preserved them as well. Later on, when there was a fear of perversion, then these *Ahadith* were compiled officially and later on, the authentic scholars gathered them together in various books. Furthermore, critics compiled a biography of all these narrators and put certain rules about how a *Hadith* could be accepted. This book includes all these details.

HUJJIYATI HADITH (URDU)

This book is regarding the authenticity of *Hadith* of the *Prophet*, as there is a baseless propaganda that *Hadith* were not written in the time of the *Prophet*, but later on, making them unreliable. This is wrong, as *Sahaba* used to write *Ahadith* and sometimes the *Prophet* himself used to order them to write. But they trusted their memory more than writing. Official compilation took place later on, when *Muslim* rulers became aware of the weakness of people's memories and the loss of those individuals writing. This book provides all these details and makes it clear that *Hadith* is *Wahi* (Revelation) and source of *Islamic Shariah* (Law).

FUNDAMENTALISM, SECULARISM AUR ISLAM (URDU)

Propaganda is being spread either because of ignorance or with mala fide intention that *Islam* is fundamentalism.

Fundamentalism was a term used for Christianity when it blocked the ways of scientific research, invention and development, and some people wanted to adopt it as a basic guideline for states and government. So those who were with research and development branded that as fundamentalism. But *Islam* does not stop or block progress and research;

rather, it encourages it and even orders scholars to go ahead and do research, as discussed in this book.

AL IJTIHADU WAT TAQLEED (URDU)

Humans are social and intellectual animals. They have all the same needs as animals, but they are distinct from them because of their intellect as they are looking for their ease, to do a little and get a lot. For this purpose, some intellectuals invent things and others follow them. Then as they are bound to obey the *Deen* of *Allah*, there are other intellectuals who deduce laws from its fundamental sources: the *Quran* and the *Sunnah*, and the less intellectuals follow them, as they should. This is the only intellectual and reasonable way. This book explains this issue and its importance.

MUSALMAN AURAT (URDU)

Allah created the world. He created humans and made them men and women. He gave different qualities to both genders for the smooth running of this life to depend upon each other, but as humans they are equal. Some women made history and they did memorable work that many men could not have done. This small book mentions some of the great work of some great women, particularly *Muslim* women, to make it clear that *Islam* deeply respects women and appreciates their contributions to society.

ASMATI RASOOL OR ZAWAJI AAISHA (URDU)

This world is a combination of opposites and some people have been given a great status. The messengers of *Allah* are the chosen and beloved of *Allah*. He made them and built them up for himself and his work. They are the most respected and honored people, and they must be given respect, as any disgrace to them can harm the feelings and sentiments of their followers, which can cause trouble. In this book this issue is discussed, as well as a misconception about the *Prophet's* marriage to *Aaisha*; namely, that she was minor at that time. Academically and research fully, this book corrects this misconception.

AL FARA'ID FIL AQA'ID (ARABIC)

Aqeedah and *Aqa'id* means faith and beliefs, respectively, and they are the base of *Deen*. Certain beliefs are the contents of *Iman*. What is important for a *Muslim* to believe? These are detailed in this concise book. Some *Muslim* sects have misconstrued some of these beliefs, so the book mentions that as well and makes the right faith clear.

QAWA'IDUT - TAJWEED (ARABIC)

One of the basic duties of the *Prophet* was to teach his followers how to recite the holy book properly. His *Sahabah* learnt it from him and then this became a specific science in future generations. They not only taught their students the proper way of recitation, they also wrote books about it. This science is called *Tajweed*, which literally means to make good, but in this science, it means to recite good. This book prescribes the basic rules for *Tajweed* as proper pronunciation not only makes the words and sounds good but also helps in giving the proper meaning of the word.

AL QAWA'IDUL FIQHIYAH *(ARABIC)*

Islam is *Deen* and a complete system and code of life. For each and every aspect of life there are rules and laws in *Islam*. Some of these rules are in text of the *Quran* and the *Sunnah*, while some others are deduced therefrom. For deduction, the authentic jurists have laid down rules of deduction and the qualities required for themselves. Then, after deduction, they have found some commonalities in different laws in different chapters, so they laid down a common rule for that and these rules called *Al Qawa'idul - Fiqhiyah*, or legal maxims, which make the study of *Fiqh* easy and understandable. This book includes some known and famous legal maxims in all four schools of jurisprudence.

AL JIHAD FIL ISLAM (ARABIC)

Jihad is a very important issue in *Islam*; to defend life, property, honor, and faith is not only a well-known right in each and every culture but also a duty in *Islam*, but how and when? This book is written on this subject; and as this issue is quite controversial, this is a reasonable answer to these questions in the light of the *Quran* and *Sunnah*.

MAULANA UBAIDULLAH SINDHI (URDU)

Maulana Ubaid Ullah Sindhi, originally from a *Sikh* family, accepted *Islam* when he was a teenager. He studied *Deen* in the proper and traditional way, then joined the freedom movement. He went through a lot of difficulties and lived in exile for 24 years. As a revolutionary leader, he is controversial, and many people wrote against him as well as for him. This book describes his personality, struggle, and thoughts to know who he was and how he was.

ASMATI RASOOL AND KHATMI NUBUWWAT (URDU)

Asmati Rasool and *Khatmi Nubuwwat* are reasonable and logical. This book consists of two parts. The defense of the *Prophet* and that of him being the last and final *Prophet* of *Allah* is a reasonable and logical thing, as *Allah* sent messengers in different times to different areas and different nations, and when they worked in their respected times in those areas, *Allah* sent the *Prophet Mohammad* to the entire world to combine their work and bring humanity together on the same theme, subject and faith that all those earlier messengers were sent for. This book is a concise, detailed, and logical interpretation of this finality.

SAYYIDAH AAISHA'S AGE AT MARRIAGE (ENGLISH)

Islam is a Natural *Deen* or *Deen* of Nature. This is a balanced *Deen* providing a comprehensive justice system, and the *Holy Prophet* is the perfect role model as a perfect human. His words, actions, and sanctions are the proper interpretation of the *Holy Quran* and the second fundamental source of laws in *Islam*. There is a commonly held belief, especially among critics of *Islam*, that the *Prophet* married *Aaisha* when she was only nine years of age. In this book, all the details about this issue are given that how this word *Tis'aa* (which means nine) happened there and what the real story is to counter the false accounts and correct the record.

JIHAD IN ISLAM: WHY, HOW, AND WHEN? (ENGLISH)

Jihad as a word in *Arabic* means struggle or striving hard, especially for a noble cause, while as a term in *Islam*, it specifically means to fight in the path/cause of *Allah*. But when does this fight happen? When it is inevitable and unavoidable as the very integrity of a state, the lives of its citizens or the very ideology is facing a big danger. But a very baseless smear campaign is going on against *Jihad* and it is branded as a synonym to terrorism, so this book is a must to make the true concept of *Jihad* clear and counter the propaganda.

SHARIA AND POLITICS *(ENGLISH)*

Islam is *Deen* and *Deen* means a complete system and a perfect code of life as this is given by the very creator of the worlds, who knows all about his creatures, their qualities, and their shortcomings, and can provide a perfect solution to their problems. But unfortunately, some people have been doing wrong in the name of *Khalafat* and presenting their wrong idea as the *Islamic* political system, so there was great need of a book that can present the proper shape of an *Islamic* state and *Islamic* political system given by the Creator; when executed properly, it is actually a mercy and blessing for the creatures. This book explains this concept clearly.

HAJJ & UMRAH IN ALL FOUR SCHOOLS OF JURISPRUDENCE *(ENGLISH)*

Hajj (pilgrimage to *Mecca*) is one of the Five Pillars of *Islam* and an especially important but a complicated type of *Ibadah* (worship) as *Muslims* from all around the world get together to perform it together. They follow the interpretation of their *Imams* (jurists), sometimes they look at others when they do not perform a specific virtue the way they do, then they think they are doing wrong, which is not so, but all of them are performing correctly according to the interpretation of their *Imams*. This book gives all these details in sequence according to all four *Imams* the *Muslim Ummah* follows.

RAMADAN: COMPONENTS OF THE HOLY MONTH (ENGLISH)

The *Islamic* Calendar is lunar based. It's different *Ibadaat* time is based on moonsighting; the lunar month starts with the new moon. Even though astronomy tells us what day the moon will be born (i.e., new) with perfect accuracy, discerning on which day it will be visible in a specific area is still not accurate. That is why differences in opinion happen all over the world, and should we to go by the calendar or by a sighting?

Also, at *Ramadan*, which is the most important month in *Islam* as a mandatory *Ibadah*, fasting is mandatory as well, but there is an extra, highly recommended *Ibadah,* the *Taraweeh*, but how many *Rakat* should we pray? *Muslims* differ about this. Another important *Ibadah* is *Salat Ul Witr*. We use this prayer all year, but during *Ramadan* this is prayed in *Jama'at,* and different *Imams* have different opinions regarding the number of *Rakats* and its procedure. So, this book gives all the details about these three prominent issues.

SCIENCE OF HADITH (ENGLISH)

Hadith is the second fundamental source of *Islamic* law. They are the words, actions, and sanctions of the *Holy Prophet*. To record all these in memory and writing, to compile it and to record the biography of those narrators who did this great job, and this is considered as a miracle of the *Prophet*. But the enemies of *Islam* used to create doubts in this regard. This book is written on this subject, and it is enough an answer to all the objections that people made from different angles.

HAJJ & UMRAH IN ALL FOUR SCHOOLS OF JURISPRUDENCE (URDU)

Hajj (pilgrimage to *Mecca*) is one of the Five Pillars of *Islam* and an especially important but a complicated type of *Ibadah* (worship) as *Muslims* from all around the world get together to perform it together. They follow the interpretation of their *Imams* (jurists), sometimes they look at others when they do not perform a specific virtue the way they do, then they think they are doing wrong, which is not so, but all of them are performing correctly according to the interpretation of their *Imams*. This book gives all these details in sequence according to all four *Imams* the *Muslim Ummah* follows.

USOOL AT - TAFSEER (PASHTO)

Every branch of science has its own rules, principles, and method-ologies, which provide guidelines for explaining it and how to interpret it, so this methodology is a circle or limits one may keep himself confines to, so he will not get lost or go astray.

This book covers the explanation of the *Holy Quran*, the last and final book of *Allah*. The book of *Allah* is the basic source of *Islam* and *Islamic* law, so its explanation requires certain rules to be followed in its explanation, so one may not be unbridled and without restraint, other-wise he will put his faith in danger.

BIDAYATUL FUHUL FI ILMIL USOOL (ARABIC)

Islamic Fiqh is "shariah" or laws of Islam. Laws are of two types substantive and procedural and all of these laws are based upon jurispru-dence. "Ilmul Usool" which is called "Ilmul Fiqh" also is the jurisprudence of "shariah." As we know that in Islam there are four fa-mous schools of jurisprudence. i.e. Hanafi, Maliki, Shafi, Hanbali. In this book the jurisprudence of all these schools are explained which can be useful for those who are interested in it. It will help them know how imams differ on certain issues.

KHUDA KAHA HAY? (URDU)

Allah placed his concept in human nature. Throughout human history people believed in Allah in one way or the other. Even agnostics as they bewilder like one who is looking for something. The atheists deny him but their denial is actually an admission that something exists but deny it. Muslims believe in Allah but there are certain issues they differ in. Its proper interpretation as to whether Allah is on the throne or is everywhere. In this book we tried to bring forth both concepts along with its proper expression as to what they meant by both.

USOOL AT - TAFSEER (URDU)

Every branch of science has its own rules, principles, and methodologies, which provide guidelines for explaining it and how to interpret it, so this methodology is a circle or limits one may keep himself confines to, so he will not get lost or go astray.

This book covers the explanation of the *Holy Quran*, the last and final book of *Allah*. The book of *Allah* is the basic source of *Islam* and *Islamic* law, so its explanation requires certain rules to be followed in its explanation, so one may not be unbridled and without restraint, otherwise he will put his faith in danger.

MOHAMMAD THE APOSTLE OF MERCY (ENGLISH)

The biography of the *Prophet Mohammad* was preserved from day one by his blessed companions. Then scholars and historians have written books in this regard in various times, both concise and detailed. This book on the biography of *Prophet Mohammad* is an excellent balance of concise and detailed, as a concise a book sometimes misses things, and people do not have time to read and understand too detailed a book. Another important feature of this book is that almost with every important part of the *Prophet's* biography, the relevant part of the *Holy Quran* has been quoted, which illustrates that the *Prophet's* life was the practical shape of the *Holy Book*.

AHSAN UL KALAM FIL A'IMMATIL AALAM (URDU)

Allah has created the world as and created therein different creatures. He created mankind as his *Khalifa* i.e. agent. He gave mankind the talent to exploit the world and the resources therein for their good, but at the same time he made him bound to follow his orders and commands. These are meant to make the life in this world a content one and prosperous in the hereafter. Allah sent mankind messengers, prophets, and books at different times. Prophet Mohammad was sent as the final messenger with the Holy Quran which he explained with words and actions. But as nature is evolutionary and the world is ephemeral which changes constantly so new issues emerge which needs solutions, so in his followers Allah blessed certain people with specific knowledge of Quran and Sunnah. They deduce and further explain these for people. These blessed people were few in number but the juristic work of four of them namely *Abu Hanifa, Malek, Shafi,* and *Ahmad* was compiled properly. These are

91

valuable assets of Islam and majority of *ummah* do follow these four jurists all over the world since their time till now.

This book *Ahsan Ul Kalam Fil A'immatil Aalam* is an introduction of these great jurists and their work in brief.

BAHLOL DANA AIK MU'AMMA SHAKHSIYAT (URDU)

Bahlol Dana is the nickname of Amr Ibni Wahab Al Kufi. He was a scholar from the Hashimite tribe. To avoid the post of judge he pretended not to be in his senses. He frequently visited Khalifa Harun and Mamun and would advise them their ministers. He would relay the issues faced by the common people and how best to address them.

He was a clever and talented individual. His lectures and words are golden but have never been compiled in a singular place according to our research. They are scattered through ought many books and we tried our best to compile them in order to gain the wisdom therein.

All those who studied the book, enjoyed its content and. The Prophet said *"the word of wisdom is the lost assets of a wise man, he deserves that wherever he found it."* So this is a word of wisdom.

IQNA -US SAAIL FI THALATHI MASA'IL (URDU)

As Muslims we are bound to worship Allah the way we have been taught and shown by the prophet Mohammad. This worship is *Fard*, *Wajib*, *Sunnah* and *Mustalab*. For certain *Ibadaat* there is a specific time and way they are to be performed. Among these *Ibadaat* prayer is the utmost important *Ibadah* and *Ramadan* is the utmost important time for *Ibadaat*.

As the lunar month starts with moon sighting and an extra ordinarily recommended prayer *Taraweeh* taking place nightly for the entire month. This prayer includes *Salati Wit'r* in congregation. In this book we have attempted to explain these three issues in the light of *Quran* and sunnah. Means 1- Moon sighting 2- *Salat Ul Taraweeh* 3- *Salat Ul Wit'r*. May *Allah* accept this effort. Ameen

ASMATI I RASOOL KHATMI NUBUWWAT AQLI AUR MANTIQI HAY (URDU)

Allah (swt) made humans bound to obey his commandments and follow his rules. For the said purpose he sent the messengers as teachers and role models. A role model has to be perfect and these he made them "maasoom" (protected). He sent Prophet Mohammad as his last and final prophet to the whole world until the last day. Allah made the Prophet extra ordinally perfect role model and ordered us to believe him as such. We are to protect and defend his finality as this is logical and reasonable.

This book is regarding this important fundamental issue. Herein this is explained logically, reasonably and textually. May Allah accept this effort. Amin!

KHULAFA E RASHIDEEN (URDU)

ABOUT THE AUTHOR

Qazi Fazl Ullah is an American philosopher, linguist, and author. He is *Fazil Wafaqul Madaris* where he studied *Arabic* grammar, *Arabic* literature, *Fiqh*, jurisprudence, logic, philosophy, *Ilmul Kalam, Seerah, Tafseer, Hadith,* and *Islamic* history. He studied at *Peshawar University* and *Islamic University Islamabad* in *Pakistan* and specialized in law, economics, and political science. He has taught all these subjects in *Pakistan* and the United States at different institutions. He was elected as a *National Assembly Parliamentarian* in *Pakistan*. He worked in underserved areas to provide jobs, build infrastructure, schools, museums, public health facilities, and increase communication technologies as the chair of the *Social Action Board*. He has traveled extensively throughout the Middle East, North Africa, Europe, Southeast Asia, North and Central America. He has given seminars in various parts of the world in these subjects. He speaks and has given lectures and seminars in *Urdu, Pashto, Farsi,* English, and *Arabic*. He has published works in *Pashto, Urdu, Arabic,* and English internationally. He has given the complete *Tafsir Ul Quran* in *Pashto* multiple times in *Pakistan*. He has also given *Tafsir Ul Quran* in *Urdu, Pashto,* and English in the United States. It includes *Usul Ul Fiqh, Usul Ul Mirath, Hadith al Qudsi, Hadith an Nabawi* in English

96

on multiple occasions. He considers himself a student to continue acquisition of knowledge. He is currently leading *Tafsir Ul Quran, Usual Al Fiqh, Seerat Un Nabi,* Science of Inheritance (*Mirath*) in English and *Al Mukhtar Lil Fatawa, Dirayat Ul Riwaya* in *Arabic* in Los Angeles, California.

www.ingramcontent.com/pod-product-compliance
Lightning Source LLC
Chambersburg PA
CBHW071916160426
42812CB00098B/1155